baby einstein®

Languages

The Walt Disney Company

Photo Credits:
Star toy courtesy of The First Years • Rooster toy courtesy of Charm Company • Robot toy courtesy of Schylling • Pig toy courtesy of Westminster • Peas photo courtesy of Bill Clark • Owl toy courtesy of Folkmanis • Horn toy courtesy of Brio

Hyperion Books for Children, New York

For information address Hyperion Books for Children, 114 Fifth Avenue, New York, New York 10011-5690.
Printed in China
Library of Congress Cataloging Card Number on file.
ISBN 0-7868-3801-9

Visit www.hyperionbooksforchildren.com and www.babyeinstein.com

Great Minds Start Little.™

star

Teaching tips

1. This is a happy star.
   What is this?

2. Sing "Twinkle, twinkle, little star" to your baby.
   Can you sing "Twinkle, twinkle, little star"?

3. We see stars in the sky at night.
   Where do we see stars?

Language lesson

English	star	STAHR
Spanish	la estrella	lah ehs-TRAY-yah
French	l'étoile	l'ay-TWAHL
German	der Stern	dare SHTAIRN
Hebrew	kokhav	koh-KHAHV
Japanese	hoshi	hoh-shee
Russian	zvezda	zviz-DAH

rooster

Teaching tips

1. Look at the rooster!
   What animal do you see?

2. A rooster says, "cock-a-doodle-do!"
   What does a rooster say?

3. A rooster is a daddy chicken.
   What do we call a daddy chicken?

Language lesson

English	rooster	ROOS-tuhr
Spanish	el gallo	el GAH-yoh
French	le coq	luh KOHK
German	der Hahn	dare HAHN
Hebrew	tarnegol	tar-neh-GOHL
Japanese	ondori	ohn-doh-ree
Russian	petukh	pi-TOOKH

robot

Teaching tips

1. This is a robot.
   Do you know what this is?

2. This robot has a red hat.
   What is the robot wearing on its head?

3. Point to parts of the robot with your baby and name them.
   Where are the robot's feet?

Language lesson

English	robot	ROH-buht
Spanish	el robot	el roh-BOHT
French	le robot	luh roh-BOH
German	der Roboter	dare roh-BOH-ter
Hebrew	robot	ROH-bot
Japanese	robotto	roh-boht-toh
Russian	robot	ROH-but

pig

Teaching tips

1. Look at the pink pig!
   What animal do you see?

2. A pig says "oink, oink!"
   What does a pig say?

3. Pigs like to roll in the mud.
   What do pigs like to do?

Language lesson

English	pig	PIG
Spanish	el cerdo	el SAIR-doh
French	le cochon	luh koh-SHONG
German	das Schwein	dahss SHVINE
Hebrew	khazir	kha-ZEER
Japanese	buta	boo-tah
Russian	svin'ya	svee-NYAH

peas

Teaching tips

1. Look at the green peas.
   What color are the peas?

2. Peas taste good.
   Do you like to eat peas?

3. Peas are vegetables.
   Can you name another vegetable?

Language lesson

English	peas	PEEZ
Spanish	los chícharos	lohss CHEE-chah-rohss
French	les pois	lay PWAH
German	die Erbsen	dee AIRP-sen
Hebrew	afunim	ah-foo-NEEM
Japanese	mame	mah-meh
Russian	gorokh	gah-ROKH

owl

Teaching tips

1. This is a white owl.
   What kind of bird is this?

2. An owl says, "whoo, whoo."
   What does an owl say?

3. Owls sleep during the day.
   When do owls sleep?

Language lesson

English	owl	OWL
Spanish	el búho	el BOO-oh
French	la chouette	lah SHWET
German	die Eule	dee OY-le
Hebrew	yanshuf	yahn-SHOOF
Japanese	fukurou	foo-koo-roh
Russian	sova	sah-VAH

lamb

Teaching tips

1. This is a white lamb.
   What animal do you see?
2. A lamb says, "baa, baa."
   What does a lamb say?
3. A lamb's fur is called wool.
   Sing "Mary Had A Little Lamb" to your baby.

Language lesson

English	lamb	LAMM
Spanish	el borrego	el bohr-RAY-goh
French	l'agneau	l'ah-NYOH
German	das Lamm	dahss LUHM
Hebrew	tale	tah-LEH
Japanese	kohitsuji	koh-hee-tsoo-jee
Russian	yagnyonok	yig-NYO-nahk

horn

Teaching tips

1. This is a horn.
   Do you know what this is?

2. A yellow bird is sitting on the horn.
   What do you see sitting on the horn?

3. When you blow a horn, it says, "toot, toot."
   What sound does a horn make?

Language lesson

English	horn	HORN
Spanish	la trompeta	lah trohm-PAY-tah
French	la trompette	lah trohm-PET
German	die Trompete	dee trohm-PAY-te
Hebrew	khatsotsra	khah-tsots-RAH
Japanese	horun	hoh-roon
Russian	rozhok	roh-ZHOK